THE CONSTITUTION EXPLAINED!

THE CONSTITUTION'S LAST FOUR ARTICLES

FROM STATES' RIGHTS TO AMENDMENTS

BY SARAH MACHAJEWSKI

Gareth Stevens PUBLISHING

Please visit our website, www.garethstevens.com. For a free color catalog of all our high-quality books, call toll free 1-800-542-2595 or fax 1-877-542-2596.

Library of Congress Cataloging-in-Publication Data

Names: Machajewski, Sarah, author.
Title: The Constitution's last four articles : from states' rights to amendments / Sarah Machajewski.
Description: New York : Gareth Stevens Publishing, [2021] | Series: The Constitution explained! | Includes bibliographical references and index.
Identifiers: LCCN 2020003507 | ISBN 9781538258644 (library binding) | ISBN 9781538258620 (paperback) | ISBN 9781538258637 (6 pack) | ISBN 9781538258651 (ebook)
Subjects: LCSH: United States. Constitution–Juvenile literature. | Constitutional history–United States–Juvenile literature. | Democracy–United States–Juvenile literature.
Classification: LCC E303 .M24 2021 | DDC 342.7302/9–dc23
LC record available at https://lccn.loc.gov/2020003507

First Edition

Published in 2021 by
Gareth Stevens Publishing
111 East 14th Street, Suite 349
New York, NY 10003

Designer: Sarah Liddell
Editor: Therese Shea

Photo credits: Cover, (main) Eliyahu Yosef Parypa/Shutterstock.com; background texture used throughout Lukasz Szwaj/Shutterstock.com; p. 5 GraphicaArtis/Contributor/Archive Photos/Getty Images; p. 7 LPETTET/E+/Getty Images; p. 9 Thorney Lieberman/Photographer's Choice/Getty Images Plus/Getty Images; p. 11 Photos.com/PHOTOS.com>>/Getty Images Plus/Getty Images; p. 13 I. Pilon/Shutterstock.com; p. 15 National Galleries of Scotland/Contributor/Hulton Fine Art Collection/Getty Images; p. 19 Bettmann/Contributor/Bettmann/Getty Images; p. 21 Education Images/Contributor/Universal Images Group/Getty Images; p. 23 Alex Wong/Staff/Getty Images News/Getty Images; p. 25 MPI/Stringer/Getty Images; p. 29 Buyenlarge/Contributor/Archive Photos/Getty Images.

Printed in the United States of America

CPSIA compliance information: Batch #CS20GS: For further information contact Gareth Stevens, New York, New York at 1-800-542-2595.

CONTENTS

WORDS IN THE GLOSSARY APPEAR IN **BOLD** TYPE THE FIRST TIME THEY ARE USED IN THE TEXT.

A DOCUMENT OF DEMOCRACY

From coast to coast, the United States is home to hundreds of millions of people, all who must obey the country's laws. Many laws are contained in the U.S. Constitution. It's one of the important **documents** in American history—perhaps the most important.

Many people are familiar with the Constitution's opening phrase: "WE THE PEOPLE . . ." It begins the preamble, or introduction, which explains the purpose of the document. Seven articles, or parts, come next, making up the main body of the Constitution. The articles establish the U.S. government and describe how it should work. They're a bit like rules that the government must follow. Even though the Constitution was written more than two centuries ago, it's still the "SUPREME LAW OF THE LAND."

A CLOSER LOOK

YOU'LL NOTICE WORDS IN THE CONSTITUTION THAT ARE SPELLED DIFFERENTLY. SOME WORDS ARE MISSPELLED. OTHERS WERE A BRITISH WAY OF SPELLING. CAPITALIZING NOUNS WAS ANOTHER STYLE AT THAT TIME.

SETTING THE TONE

At 52 words, the powerful preamble of the Constitution tells the world that the United States is one nation and that its laws belong to its citizens. It also identifies why this set of laws was established: "IN ORDER TO FORM A MORE PERFECT UNION, ESTABLISH JUSTICE, INSURE DOMESTIC [NATIONAL] TRANQUILITY [PEACE], PROVIDE FOR THE COMMON DEFENCE, PROMOTE THE GENERAL WELFARE, AND SECURE THE BLESSINGS OF LIBERTY TO OURSELVES AND OUR POSTERITY [FUTURE GENERATIONS]."

THE CONSTITUTION WAS WRITTEN IN 1787 AT THE CONSTITUTIONAL **CONVENTION**, A MEETING OF LEADERS HOPING TO STRENGTHEN THE YOUNG NATION.

MAKING SENSE OF THE CONSTITUTION

All power of the federal, or national, government comes from the Constitution. Yet, while the Constitution gives the government power, it also limits this power. The limitations protect the rights of U.S. citizens as well as the rights of the state governments. This careful balance allows the federal government to act and make decisions for the country while respecting people's freedoms and the powers of the state governments.

The Constitution has key defining features. It established three branches of government, called the legislative, executive, and **judicial** branches. Its built-in system of checks and balances keeps one branch from becoming too powerful. The document also establishes the relationships between the states. Finally, the Constitution outlines a process for how the document can be amended, which means changed or added to.

A CLOSER LOOK

THE SEVEN ARTICLES OF THE CONSTITUTION ARE NUMBERED WITH ROMAN NUMERALS. THIS BOOK FOCUSES ON THE LAST FOUR ARTICLES, WHICH ARE NUMBERED IV (4), V (5), VI (6), AND VII (7).

A NEW LAW OF THE LAND

The United States' first set of national laws was called the Articles of Confederation. These laws gave power to the states, but created a weak central government. The states fought over things like taxes and territory, and the national government had no power to enforce laws. Leaders worried the young nation could fall apart just a few years after it had been established. Attempts to improve the Articles of Confederation led to the creation of the Constitution.

THE CONSTITUTION'S MAIN PARTS ARE THE PREAMBLE, THE ARTICLES, AND THE AMENDMENTS. THE FIRST 10 AMENDMENTS ARE KNOWN AS THE BILL OF RIGHTS.

...be held in the State where the said Crimes shall ... such Place or Places as the Congress may by Law have directed.
... only in levying War against them, or in adhering to their Enemies, giving them Aid and Comfort. ... unless on the Testimony of two Witnesses to the same overt Act, or on Confession in open Court.
The Congress shall have Power to declare the Punishment of Treason, but no Attainder of Treason shall work Corruption of Blood, or Forfeiture except during the Life of the Person attainted.

Article IV.

Section. 1. Full Faith and Credit shall be given in each State to the public Acts, Records, and judicial Proceedings of every other State. And the Congress may by general Laws prescribe the Manner in which such Acts, Records and Proceedings shall be proved, and the Effect thereof.

Section. 2. The Citizens of each State shall be entitled to all Privileges and Immunities of Citizens in the several States.

A Person charged in any State with Treason, Felony, or other Crime, who shall flee from Justice, and be found in another State, shall on Demand of the executive Authority of the State from which he fled, be delivered up, to be removed to the State having Jurisdiction of the Crime.

No Person held to Service or Labour in one State, under the Laws thereof, escaping into another, shall, in Consequence of any Law or Regulation therein, be discharged from such Service or Labour, but shall be delivered up on Claim of the Party to whom such Service or Labour may be due.

Section. 3. New States may be admitted by the Congress into this Union; but no new State shall be formed or erected within the Jurisdiction of any other State; nor any State be formed by the Junction of two or more States, or Parts of States, without the Consent of the Legislatures of the States concerned as well as of the Congress.

The Congress shall have Power to dispose of and make all needful Rules and Regulations respecting the Territory or other Property belonging to the United States; and nothing in this Constitution shall be so construed as to Prejudice any Claims of the United States, or of any particular State.

Section. 4. The United States shall guarantee to every State in this Union a Republican Form of Government, and shall protect each of them against Invasion; and on Application of the Legislature, or of the Executive (when the Legislature cannot be convened) against domestic Violence.

Article. V.

The Congress, whenever two thirds of both Houses shall deem it necessary, shall propose Amendments to this Constitution, or, on the Application of the Legislatures of two thirds of the several States, shall call a Convention for proposing Amendments, which, in either Case, shall be valid to all Intents and Purposes, as Part of this Constitution, when ratified by the Legislatures of three fourths of the several States, or by Conventions in three fourths thereof, as the one or the other Mode of Ratification may be proposed by the Congress; Provided that no Amendment which may be made prior to the Year One thousand eight hundred and eight shall in any Manner affect the first and fourth Clauses in the Ninth Section of the first Article; and that no State, without its Consent, shall be deprived of its equal Suffrage in the Senate.

Article. VI.

All Debts contracted and Engagements entered into, before the Adoption of this Constitution, shall be as valid against the United States under this Constitution, as under the Confederation.

This Constitution, and the Laws of the United States which shall be made in Pursuance thereof; and all Treaties made, or which shall be made, under the Authority of the United States, shall be the supreme Law of the Land; and the Judges in every State shall be bound thereby, any Thing in the Constitution or Laws of any State to the Contrary notwithstanding.

The Senators and Representatives before mentioned, and the Members of the several State Legislatures, and all executive and judicial Officers, both of the United States and of the several States, shall be bound by Oath or Affirmation, to support this Constitution; but no religious Test shall ever be required as a Qualification to any Office or public Trust under the United States.

Article. VII.

The Ratification of the Conventions of nine States, shall be sufficient for the Establishment of this Constitution between the States so ratifying the Same.

tion by the Unanimous Consent of the States present the Seventeenth

THE RELATIONSHIP BETWEEN THE STATES

When the Constitution was written, the states had been united as one country for just 11 years. The states had differing laws and politics. The Constitution addressed these differences by defining the relationships between the states. Article IV Section 1 declares, **"FULL FAITH AND CREDIT SHALL BE GIVEN IN EACH STATE TO THE PUBLIC ACTS, RECORDS, AND JUDICIAL PROCEEDINGS OF EVERY OTHER STATE."** This means every state must respect other states' laws, records, and court decisions.

Article IV Section 1 then says, **"THE CONGRESS MAY BY GENERAL LAWS PRESCRIBE THE MANNER IN WHICH SUCH ACTS, RECORDS AND PROCEEDINGS SHALL BE PROVED, AND THE EFFECT THEREOF."** Congress has the power to get involved when state laws are different. A federal law may direct states to handle their differences in a certain way.

A CLOSER LOOK

LAWS ABOUT CRIME, MARRIAGE AND DIVORCE, REAL ESTATE, GAMBLING, AND GUN CONTROL ARE EXAMPLES OF LAWS MADE AT THE STATE LEVEL. THESE LAWS MAY BE OUTLINED IN STATE CONSTITUTIONS.

STATES' RIGHTS

All states have to follow federal laws, but they have the right to make their own laws about certain subjects too, such as gambling. People travel freely between states all the time. What if a legal decision made in one state is illegal in another? Article IV tells us states must honor laws and judicial decisions made in other states. For example, Kansas has to recognize the adoption of a child that took place in New York.

WHEN STATE LAWS ARE IN CONFLICT, THE FEDERAL GOVERNMENT HAS THE POWER TO DECIDE WHAT THE COURSE OF ACTION SHOULD BE. WHEN STATE LAW CONFLICTS WITH FEDERAL LAW, FEDERAL LAW ALWAYS HAS MORE POWER.

EQUAL TREATMENT AND EXTRADITION

Article IV Section 2 says, **"THE CITIZENS OF EACH STATE SHALL BE ENTITLED TO ALL PRIVILEGES AND IMMUNITIES OF CITIZENS IN THE SEVERAL STATES."** A citizen must be treated like a citizen of a state even if it's not their home. Today, U.S. citizens are used to receiving equal treatment across states for the most part. However, back when the nation was established, there were fears each state would operate as a separate nation.

Article IV Section 2 requires that states return people who have been charged with a crime **"TO THE STATE HAVING JURISDICTION OF THE CRIME,"** or the state where the crime was said to have been committed. This action is called extradition, and this section, called the extradition **clause**, means states must help each other enforce certain laws.

A CLOSER LOOK

THE WORDS "SLAVE" AND "SLAVERY" DON'T APPEAR IN ARTICLE IV OR THE REST OF THE CONSTITUTION. ABOLITIONIST AND FORMER SLAVE FREDERICK DOUGLASS SAID, "ABOLISH SLAVERY TOMORROW, AND NOT A SENTENCE OR **SYLLABLE** OF THE CONSTITUTION NEED BE ALTERED."

THE FUGITIVE SLAVE CLAUSE

Slavery was legal in some states when the Constitution was written. Many enslaved black people attempted to flee to states where slavery was illegal so they could be free. However, Article IV Section 2 of the Constitution required states to return anyone "HELD TO SERVICE OR LABOUR" who escaped into another state. This was known as the fugitive slave clause. This clause lost its power after the Thirteenth Amendment outlawed slavery in 1865.

THE FUGITIVE SLAVE CLAUSE OF THE CONSTITUTION ALLOWED ESCAPED SLAVES TO BE CAPTURED IN THE NORTH AND RETURNED TO THE SOUTH. IT ALSO PAVED THE WAY FOR THOUSANDS OF FREE BLACKS TO BE KIDNAPPED AND SOLD INTO SLAVERY.

FREDERICK DOUGLASS

NEW STATES AND TERRITORIES

Article IV Section 3 addresses the growth of the United States, allowing for new states to join. It says: "NEW STATES MAY BE ADMITTED BY THE CONGRESS INTO THIS UNION; BUT NO NEW STATE SHALL BE FORMED OR ERECTED WITHIN THE JURISDICTION OF ANY OTHER STATE; NOR ANY STATE BE FORMED BY THE JUNCTION OF TWO OR MORE STATES, OR PARTS OF STATES, WITHOUT THE CONSENT OF THE LEGISLATURES OF THE STATES CONCERNED AS WELL AS OF THE CONGRESS." Basically, this means states don't need to worry about losing land to the formation of new states unless they agree to it.

Article IV Section 3 also gives Congress authority over U.S. territories and to make "ALL NEEDFUL RULES AND REGULATIONS RESPECTING THE TERRITORY."

STATE DIVISION

States have formed out of territory from other states. Maine was once part of Massachusetts. Massachusetts agreed to allow Maine to form its own state, which occurred in 1820. West Virginia was a part of Virginia before the American Civil War. When Virginia broke away from the United States in 1861, counties that disagreed with the decision formed a legislature. It was this state government that consented to become a new state, as required by Article IV Section 3.

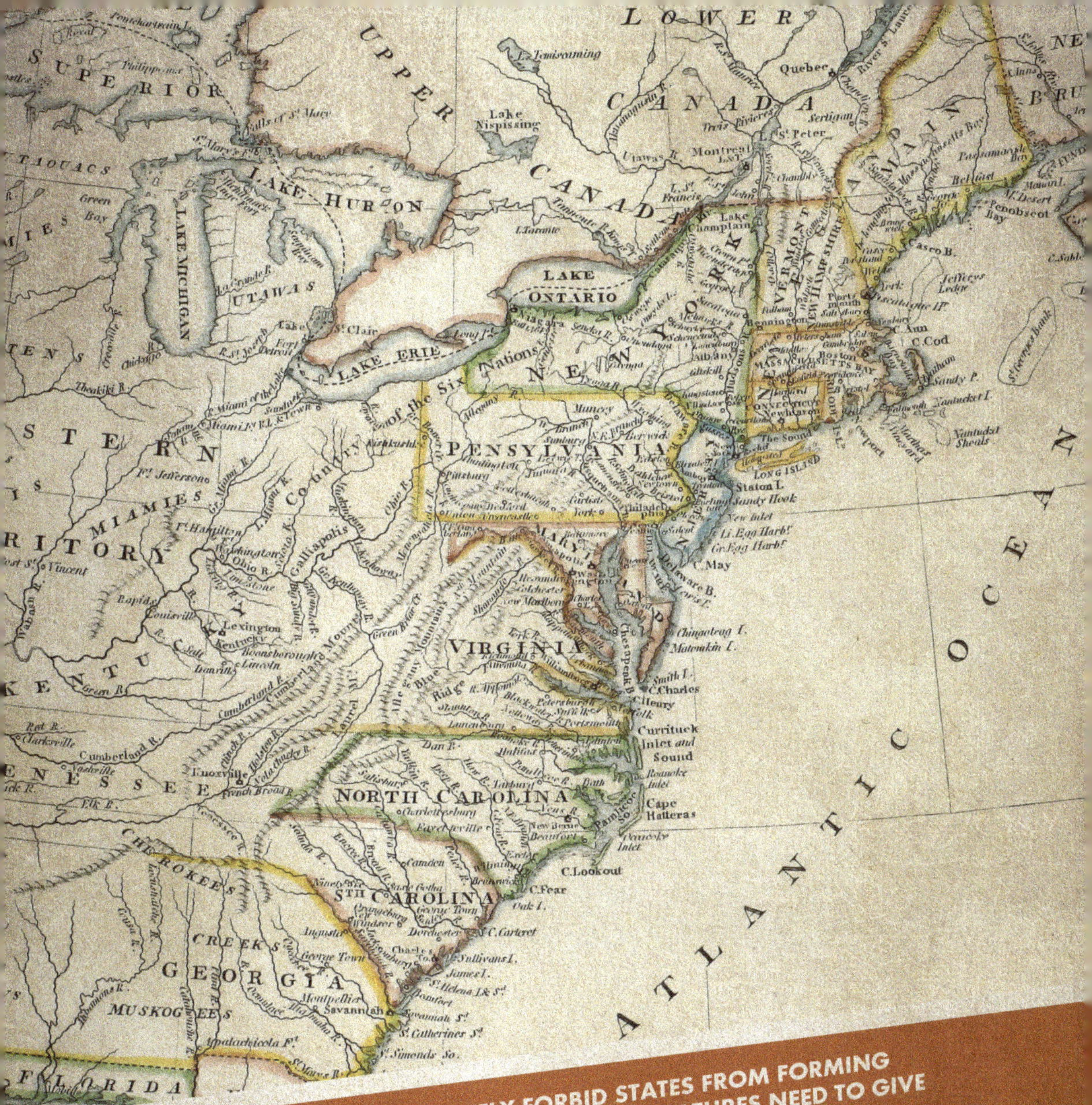

ARTICLE IV DOESN'T COMPLETELY FORBID STATES FROM FORMING FROM OTHER STATES. IT SAYS THE STATE LEGISLATURES NEED TO GIVE CONSENT IN ORDER FOR THAT TO HAPPEN.

A CLOSER LOOK

MOST STATES HAVE JOINED THE UNITED STATES AFTER BEING TERRITORIES FIRST, AND WERE THEREFORE UNDER THE CONTROL OF CONGRESS. CONGRESS HAS THIS POWER BECAUSE OF ARTICLE IV SECTION 3.

PROMISES AND PROTECTION

Article IV Section 4 declares, **"THE UNITED STATES SHALL GUARANTEE TO EVERY STATE IN THIS UNION A REPUBLICAN FORM OF GOVERNMENT."** A republican government is one in which citizens have the power. They exercise this power by voting for officials and representatives who act on their behalf. Therefore, a state government couldn't set itself up as a monarchy or any kind of ruling body that didn't allow elections.

This section also promises the states that the federal government **"SHALL PROTECT EACH OF THEM AGAINST INVASION; AND ON APPLICATION OF THE LEGISLATURE, OR OF THE EXECUTIVE (WHEN THE LEGISLATURE CANNOT BE CONVENED [ASSEMBLED]) AGAINST DOMESTIC VIOLENCE."** This means federal forces can enter states to protect them against invasions or to restore peace when violence breaks out domestically, or within the nation.

A CLOSER LOOK

FOUNDING FATHER ALEXANDER HAMILTON PROPOSED THAT THE U.S. PRESIDENT SERVE FOR LIFE. THAT WAS TOO MUCH LIKE A KING FOR MANY OTHER LEADERS. THE IDEA WAS REJECTED QUICKLY.

A KING NEVER AGAIN

Rule by monarchy is against the founding principles of the United States. Article IV Section 4 guarantees that no state will ever be ruled by a king. The Constitution's writers may have feared that a monarchy in a state could threaten other states' governments and even the nation as a whole. The former British colonies fought for independence from the British monarchy. The protection written into the Constitution assures the country can never return to that form of government.

DURING THE AMERICAN REVOLUTION (1775–1783), GEORGE III WAS THE KING OF GREAT BRITAIN. AMERICAN LEADERS DIDN'T WANT TO LIVE UNDER THIS KIND OF GOVERNMENT AGAIN, WHICH IS WHY ARTICLE IV SECTION 4 GUARANTEES A REPUBLICAN GOVERNMENT IN EVERY STATE.

AMENDING THE CONSTITUTION

The writers of the Constitution, called its framers, understood that changes or additions to it might be necessary as years went by. The process for making changes to the Constitution is in Article V.

Article V states, **"THE CONGRESS, WHENEVER TWO THIRDS OF BOTH HOUSES SHALL DEEM [BELIEVE] IT NECESSARY, SHALL PROPOSE AMENDMENTS TO THIS CONSTITUTION."** This means Congress can propose an amendment when two-thirds of the members of the Senate and two-thirds of the members of the House of Representatives agree to it. Then, the state legislatures—or special state conventions—vote on the amendment. Article V says that an amendment is ratified, or officially approved, if **"LEGISLATURES OF THREE FOURTHS OF THE SEVERAL STATES, OR BY CONVENTIONS IN THREE FOURTHS THEREOF"** vote in favor of it.

A CLOSER LOOK

ACCORDING TO ARTICLE V, NO AMENDMENT CAN DENY A STATE'S **"EQUAL SUFFRAGE,"** OR RIGHT TO VOTE, IN THE SENATE.

ANOTHER CHANCE FOR CHANGE

Every amendment to the U.S. Constitution to date has been proposed using the two-thirds process of Congress described in this chapter. However, Article V provides one more way for amendments to be proposed, though it has never been used: "LEGISLATURES OF TWO THIRDS OF THE SEVERAL STATES, SHALL CALL A CONVENTION FOR PROPOSING AMENDMENTS." However, these amendments still need to be approved by three-fourths of the states after that.

WHAT DO THESE FRACTIONS MEAN TODAY? TWO-THIRDS OF THE SENATE IS 67 SENATORS. TWO-THIRDS OF THE HOUSE OF REPRESENTATIVES IS 290 REPRESENTATIVES. TWO-THIRDS OF THE STATES IS 34 STATES. THREE-FOURTHS OF THE STATES IS 38.

HOW TO PASS AN AMENDMENT

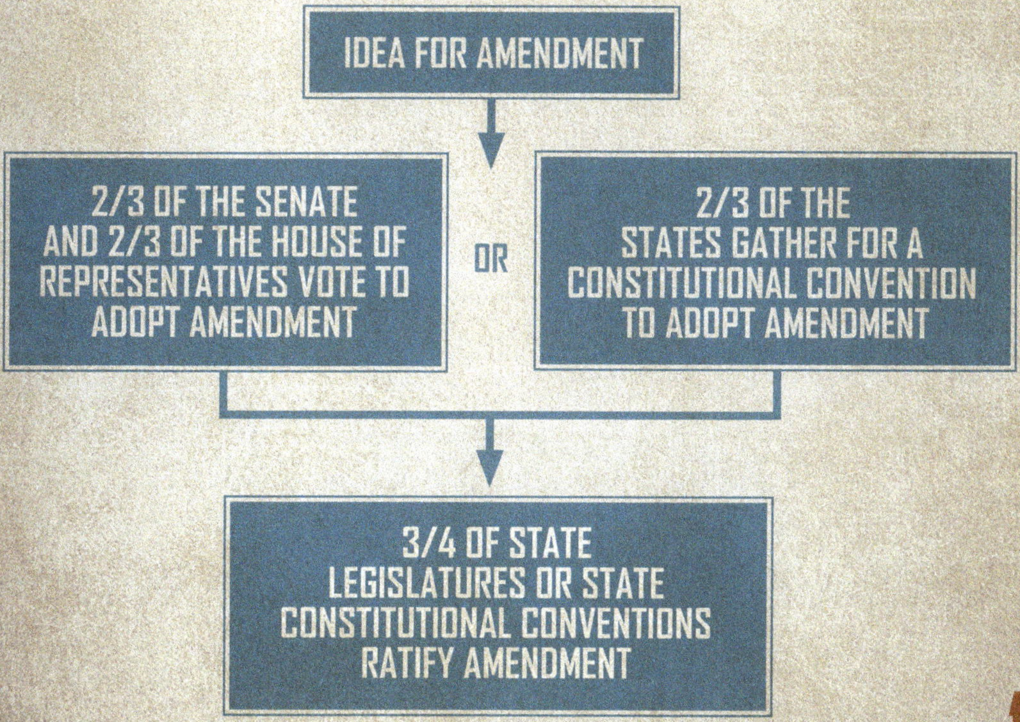

KEY MOMENTS OF CHANGE

While the process of proposing and ratifying an amendment seems simple, it is difficult in practice. Only 27 amendments have passed although the Constitution has been in operation for more than two centuries.

The first 10 amendments, the Bill of Rights, passed just three years after the Constitution itself was ratified. These amendments protect many important civil rights, like freedom of speech and religion, as well as limit the power of the federal government.

Many amendments that follow the Bill of Rights reflect key moments in American history. The Thirteenth Amendment abolished slavery in 1865, at the end of the Civil War. The Nineteenth Amendment gave women the right to vote in 1920. The Twenty-sixth Amendment lowered the voting age from 21 to 18 in 1971.

A CLOSER LOOK

THE TENTH AMENDMENT STATES THAT ANY POWERS NOT GIVEN TO THE FEDERAL GOVERNMENT **"ARE RESERVED TO THE STATES RESPECTIVELY [INDIVIDUALLY], OR TO THE PEOPLE."**

"HEREBY REPEALED"

What happens if an amendment doesn't fit what the country wants? Another change is needed, and the process outlined in Article V is followed once more. Passed in 1919, the Eighteenth Amendment made manufacturing, selling, and transporting alcohol illegal. It lasted 14 years. In 1933, the Eighteenth Amendment was repealed, or officially ended, with the passage of the Twenty-first Amendment. It states, "THE EIGHTEENTH ARTICLE OF AMENDMENT TO THE CONSTITUTION OF THE UNITED STATES IS HEREBY REPEALED."

THE TWENTY-SECOND AMENDMENT, RATIFIED IN 1951, LIMITED THE NUMBER OF TERMS A PRESIDENT CAN SERVE TO TWO. THIS CHANGE FOLLOWED FRANKLIN DELANO ROOSEVELT'S PRESIDENCY. ROOSEVELT HAD BEEN ELECTED FOUR TIMES.

THE SUPREMACY CLAUSE

Some sections of the Constitution give power specifically to the federal government or to the state governments. Other sections simply address issues that may occur as the levels of government interact. One issue the framers **anticipated** was that state laws would sometimes come into conflict with national laws. Article VI of the Constitution tells the courts what to do when this happens.

Called the supremacy clause, it says, "THIS CONSTITUTION, AND THE LAWS OF THE UNITED STATES . . . AND ALL TREATIES MADE, OR WHICH SHALL BE MADE, UNDER THE AUTHORITY OF THE UNITED STATES, SHALL BE THE SUPREME LAW OF THE LAND, AND THE JUDGES IN EVERY STATE SHALL BE BOUND THEREBY." When state laws and federal laws conflict, federal law has more power.

A CLOSER LOOK

THE U.S. SUPREME COURT DETERMINES IF THERE'S A DISAGREEMENT BETWEEN STATE AND FEDERAL LAWS. THE SUPREMACY CLAUSE EMPOWERS THIS BRANCH OF THE GOVERNMENT.

RELATIONS WITH TRIBAL NATIONS

The U.S. Constitution recognizes tribal nations as sovereign governments. This means that tribal nations have the right to self-government; they operate independently from the United States. According to many treaties signed by tribal nations and the U.S. government, the federal government has a responsibility to protect the concept of self-government. Article VI supports these treaties, stating, "THIS CONSTITUTION . . . AND ALL TREATIES MADE . . . SHALL BE THE SUPREME LAW OF THE LAND."

INDIAN RESERVATIONS ARE LOCATED WITHIN U.S. STATES. TRIBAL GOVERNMENTS OWN AND GOVERN THIS LAND, SO STATES HAVE NO POWER TO ENFORCE LAWS THERE. IF THEY TRIED, THEY WOULD BE IN VIOLATION OF ARTICLE VI OF THE CONSTITUTION.

NO RELIGIOUS TESTS

A fundamental principle of U.S. law is the separation between church and state. It means that the government (the "state") cannot interfere with religion (the "church"). Religions can't get involved with the government either. This famous phrase isn't found in the Constitution, but the document does address this idea in a few sections. Article VI contains what is known as the no religious test clause.

It begins by stating that all government officials, such as senators, representatives, and judges, have to swear an oath to support the Constitution. Then it continues, **"BUT NO RELIGIOUS TEST SHALL EVER BE REQUIRED AS A QUALIFICATION TO ANY OFFICE."** This language was meant to protect officials from religious **discrimination** based on their beliefs.

A CLOSER LOOK

THE FAMOUS PHRASE "SEPARATION OF CHURCH AND STATE" COMES FROM A LETTER WRITTEN BY THOMAS JEFFERSON IN 1802.

PROTECTING FREEDOM OF RELIGION

Religious discrimination was a common practice in England and occurred in U.S. states around the time of the Constitution's writing. Religious tests were used to keep people of some religions from holding office. The Constitution used the power of law to stop this practice in the federal government. The idea that religious discrimination is unlawful is found later in the Constitution in the First Amendment. It protects people's right to practice any religion—or no religion—without fear.

THE SEPARATENESS OF GOVERNMENT AND RELIGION IS AN IMPORTANT PART OF THE CONSTITUTION. IN THIS PICTURE, PROTESTORS HOLD UP SIGNS RELATED TO THIS IDEA.

THE LAST ARTICLE

The last article of the Constitution is Article VII. Without this article, the shortest in the document, there might be no Constitution. Article VII explains the process of ratification for the Constitution in just one sentence: **"THE RATIFICATION OF THE CONVENTIONS OF NINE STATES, SHALL BE SUFFICIENT FOR THE ESTABLISHMENT OF THIS CONSTITUTION BETWEEN THE STATES SO RATIFYING THE SAME."**

Article VII simply outlines a process. In order for the Constitution to pass and become the law of the land, nine states had to ratify it through state conventions—not state legislatures. The framers feared that state legislatures wouldn't ratify the document, since the Constitution required that the states lose some power in order to form a stronger federal government.

A CLOSER LOOK

IN ARTICLE VII, THE NUMBER NINE IS SAID TO BE **"SUFFICIENT,"** BECAUSE IT WAS A MAJORITY OF WHAT WAS THEN 13 STATES. IN THIS CASE, MAJORITY MEANS "A NUMBER THAT IS GREATER THAN HALF OF A TOTAL."

ENSURING RATIFICATION

The Articles of Confederation had outlined a process for making changes to it. A section of that document required that all state legislatures needed to support amendments. This made changes very difficult; just one state could prevent amendments from passing. The framers chose to replace the Articles, rather than present the Constitution as a change to it. So, the new Constitution only required the approval of nine states, which made its passage much more likely.

THE U.S. GOVERNMENT OPERATED UNDER THE ARTICLES OF CONFEDERATION FROM 1781 TO 1789.

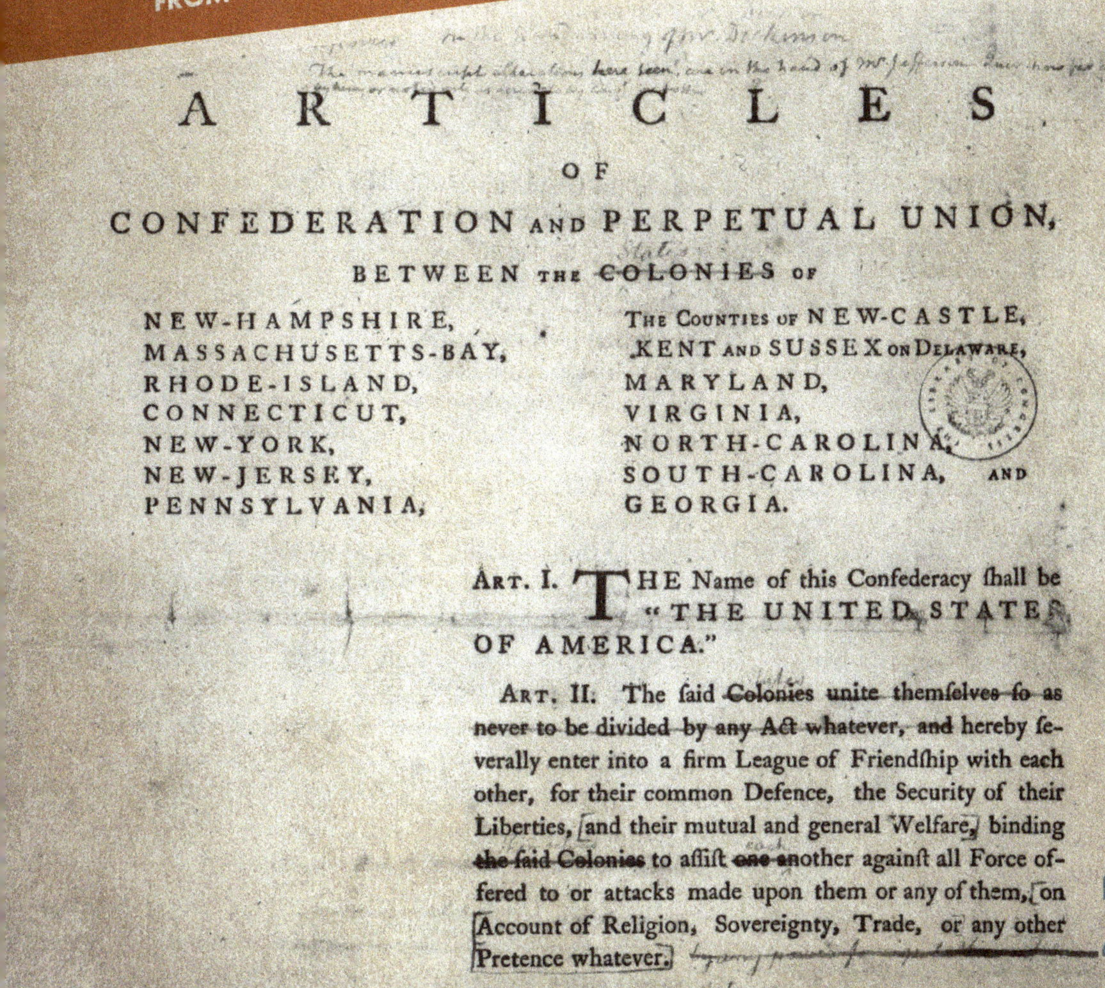

A R T I C L E S

OF

CONFEDERATION AND PERPETUAL UNION,

BETWEEN THE COLONIES OF

NEW-HAMPSHIRE, MASSACHUSETTS-BAY, RHODE-ISLAND, CONNECTICUT, NEW-YORK, NEW-JERSEY, PENNSYLVANIA, THE COUNTIES OF NEW-CASTLE, KENT AND SUSSEX ON DELAWARE, MARYLAND, VIRGINIA, NORTH-CAROLINA, SOUTH-CAROLINA, AND GEORGIA.

ART. I. THE Name of this Confederacy ſhall be "THE UNITED STATES OF AMERICA."

ART. II. The ſaid Colonies unite themſelves ſo as never to be divided by any Act whatever, and hereby ſeverally enter into a firm League of Friendſhip with each other, for their common Defence, the Security of their Liberties, and their mutual and general Welfare, binding the ſaid Colonies to aſſiſt one another againſt all Force offered to or attacks made upon them or any of them, on Account of Religion, Sovereignty, Trade, or any other Pretence whatever.

THE ROAD TO RATIFICATION

For a document that has been such a key part of the American identity, the road to ratification wasn't smooth. The Constitutional Convention met for months, **debating** and questioning the ideas that would govern the young nation. Some states believed the Constitution didn't protect individual liberties and refused to support it. James Madison wrote amendments, which became the Bill of Rights, to answer this concern.

In December 1787, Delaware became the first state to ratify the new Constitution. In 1788, New Hampshire became the ninth state to ratify it, making the Constitution law. All 13 states ratified the Constitution by 1790, almost three years after the original draft was written. In 1791, the Bill of Rights was ratified according to the ratification process in Article V.

A CLOSER LOOK

JAMES MADISON PRESENTED 19 AMENDMENTS TO CONGRESS. IN THE END, 10 WERE RATIFIED. MORE THAN 11,000 AMENDMENTS HAVE BEEN PROPOSED IN ALL!

ATTEMPTS TO AMEND ARTICLE V

The U.S. Congress website lists proposals under consideration. In 2016, the website outlined a suggestion for a new amendment. It would change Article V by only allowing a constitutional convention to vote on proposing one new amendment at a time. The concern was that just one convention could lead to significant changes to the Constitution. While this amendment hasn't been passed, the attempt shows continuing interest in the Constitution's language and ideas.

THE CONSTITUTION MAY NOT HAVE BEEN RATIFIED WITHOUT THE PROMISE OF A BILL OF RIGHTS. MASSACHUSETTS, FOR EXAMPLE, NARROWLY RATIFIED IT ONLY AFTER THE ADDITION OF THE BILL OF RIGHTS WAS PROMISED.

TIMELINE TO RATIFICATION

DECEMBER 7, 1787: DELAWARE
DECEMBER 12, 1787: PENNSYLVANIA
DECEMBER 18, 1787: NEW JERSEY
JANUARY 2, 1788: GEORGIA
JANUARY 9, 1788: CONNECTICUT
FEBRUARY 6, 1788: MASSACHUSETTS
APRIL 28, 1788: MARYLAND
MAY 23, 1788: SOUTH CAROLINA
JUNE 21, 1788: NEW HAMPSHIRE
JUNE 25, 1788: VIRGINIA
JULY 26, 1788: NEW YORK
NOVEMBER 21, 1789: NORTH CAROLINA
MAY 29, 1790: RHODE ISLAND

→ THE U.S. CONSTITUTION IS RATIFIED.

WRITTEN TO LAST

If you pay attention to the news, you'll discover that the Constitution makes headlines nearly every day. Both the state and federal governments use the Constitution when creating new state and federal laws. If these laws are interpreted to be unconstitutional—or against the Constitution—the U.S. Supreme Court can strike them down. Governments and courts use the articles' language as roadmaps for other decisions and actions too. The document doesn't contain suggestions. It contains instructions that must be followed.

American history shows that the Constitution was built to last. Its words shaped a strong but **flexible** foundation for the nation. The amendments have allowed the Constitution to grow and change as the country has grown and changed. The U.S. Constitution remains as vital today as it was more than two centuries ago.

UPHOLDING THE CONSTITUTION

The Supreme Court is the highest court in the judicial branch of the U.S. government. Article III of the Constitution created the Supreme Court and also gives it its power. The court has many key responsibilities. It interprets and sometimes oversees the laws and actions of the other branches of government. It also limits the other branches' power. The Supreme Court works to protect civil rights guaranteed by the Constitution too.

THE CONSTITUTION'S FOUR PAGES ARE ON DISPLAY FOR ALL TO SEE IN WASHINGTON, DC.

A CLOSER LOOK

IN 2015, THE U.S. SUPREME COURT RULED THAT MARRIAGE EQUALITY IS PROTECTED UNDER THE FOURTEENTH AMENDMENT, WHICH GUARANTEES ALL CITIZENS EQUAL PROTECTION UNDER THE LAW. THIS IS AN EXAMPLE OF ARTICLE VI, THE SUPREMACY CLAUSE, AT WORK.

GLOSSARY

anticipate: to expect or predict

clause: a specific part of a legal document

convention: a gathering of people who have a common interest or purpose

debate: having to do with formal public discussion or argument

discrimination: unfairly treating people unequally because of their race or beliefs

document: a formal piece of writing

flexible: capable of changing to adapt to new situations

guarantee: to promise

immunity: protection from something

judicial: having to do with courts of law and judges

jurisdiction: the area over which laws can be enforced

prescribe: to make a rule

syllable: an individual sound that makes up a word or part of a word in spoken language

violation: the act of ignoring someone's rights. Also, the act of breaking a law.

FOR MORE INFORMATION

BOOKS

Conley, Kate. *12 Questions About the US Constitution.* Mankato, MN: 12-Story Library, 2016.

Mooney, Carla. *The U.S. Constitution: Discover How Democracy Works.* White River Junction, VT: Nomad Press, 2016.

Travis, Cathy. *Constitution Translated for Kids.* Washington, DC: CT Bookshelf, 2016.

WEBSITES

The Constitution
www.ducksters.com/history/us_constitution.php
Learn more about the writing of the Constitution, including alternate ideas.

The Constitution of the United States
www.archives.gov/founding-docs/constitution
Explore the Constitution and view pictures of it.

INDEX